The bluebird carries the sky on his back.
—HENRY DAVID THOREAU (1817–1862)
American writer and naturalist

Running Press Book Publishers, 125 South Twenty-second Street, Philadelphia, Pennsylvania 19103.

THE
BIRD
LOVER'S
JOURNAL

Look for birds with your ears.
—WILLIAM E. SAUNDERS
20th–century Canadian naturalist and writer

In order to see birds it is necessary to become a part of the silence.

—ROBERT LYND (1879–1949)
Irish journalist

...two robins are tapping at my window now, and I've never been
able to resist their invitation.

—LEN EISERER, b. 1948
American writer and professor of psychology

It is the liquid notes of a river that we hear in a robin's song.

—T.H. WHITE (1906–1964)
English writer

Birds are to see, to hear, to store in memory.

—ALLAN D. CRUICKSHANK (1907–1974)
American lecturer, editor, and writer

The greatest threat to our birds today no longer is the man with the gun, but the man with the bulldozer and dump truck.

—HENRY HILL COLLINS, JR.
20th-century American naturalist

...birds are far more than robins, thrushes, and finches to brighten the suburban garden, or ducks and grouse to fill the sportsman's bag, or rare waders or warblers to be ticked off on a bird watcher's checklist. They are indicators of the environment—a sort of environmental litmus-paper.

—ROGER TORY PETERSON, b. 1908
American ornithologist

...the first written verse in the English language was in praise
of a beloved bird.

—JOHN KIERAN (1892–1981)
American writer

Every human being looks to the birds. They suit the fancy of us all. What they feel they can voice, as we try to; they court and nest, they battle with the elements, they are torn by two opposing impulses, a love of home and a passion for far places. Only with birds do we share so much emotion.

—DONALD CULROSS PEATTIE (1898–1964)
American naturalist

A question frequently heard, especially from persons trying to make conversation, is, "How did you first become interested in birds?" Strangely enough, this question is seldom asked among birders themselves.

—ROGER BARTON (1903–1976)
American advertising expert, lecturer and writer

*For most bird-watchers, the coming of the warblers has the
same effect as catnip on a cat.*

—ARLINE THOMAS, b. 1913
American writer

Of all the wild creatures that persist in New England, the Loon seems best to typify the stark wildness of primeval nature.

—E.H. FORBUSH
20th-century American naturalist

A sparrow fluttering about the church is an antagonist which the most profound theologian. . .is wholly unable to overcome.

—SYDNEY SMITH (1771–1845)
English clergyman and essayist

The ousel-cock so black of hue,
  With orange-tawny bill,
The throstle, with his not so true,
  The wren with little quill.
—WILLIAM SHAKESPEARE (1564–1616)
English dramatist and poet

To test our eyes we often watched a lark until he seemed a faint speck in the sky. . .and still the music came pouring down to us in glorious profusion, from a height far above our vision.

—JOHN MUIR (1838–1914)
American naturalist

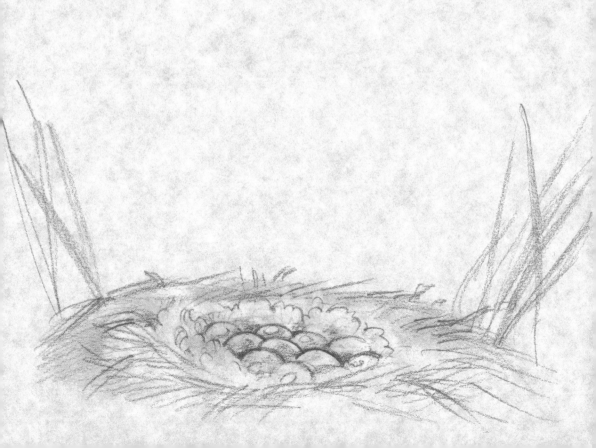

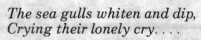

The sea gulls whiten and dip,
Crying their lonely cry....
—ARTHUR SYMONS (1865–1945)
English poet and critic

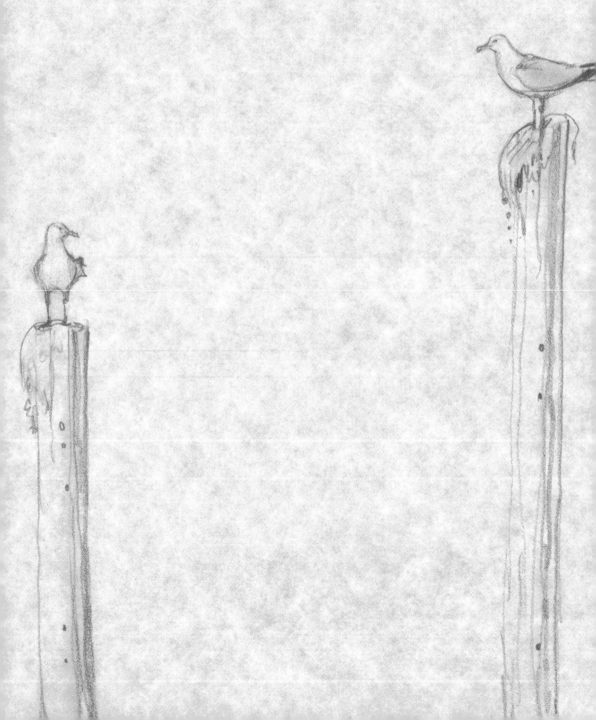

. . .we judge bird song not by its musical quality nor even by its creativeness, but by its effect on the human spirit.

—LEN EISERER, b. 1948
American writer and professor of psychology

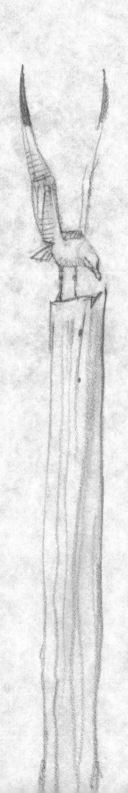

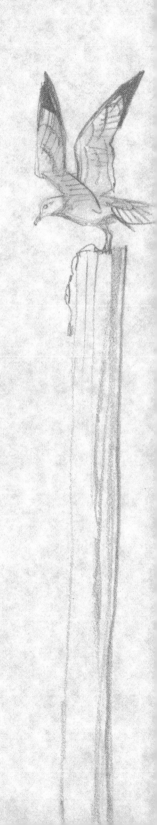

It is not art that rains down upon us in the song of a bird; but the simplest modulation, correctly executed, is already art.

—IGOR STRAVINSKY (1882–1971)
Russian-born American composer

When a nightingale sits up all night singing to his wife, and singing very well, too, you can't make me believe that aesthetic values of a very high order are not present.

—ALFRED NORTH WHITEHEAD (1861-1947)
English mathematician and philosopher

The restlessness of shorebirds, their kinship with the distance and swift seasons, the wistful signal of their voices down the long coastlines of the world make them, for me, the most affecting of wild creatures.

—PETER MATTHIESSEN, b. 1927
American naturalist and writer

Even when the bird walks one feels that it has wings.
—ANTOINE-MARIN LEMIERRE (1733–1793)
French writer

The little birds of the field have God for their caterer.
—MIGUEL DE CERVANTES (1547–1616)
Spanish writer

It is astonishing how violently a big branch shakes when a silly little bird has left it. I expect the bird knows it and feels immensely arrogant.

—KATHERINE MANSFIELD (1888–1924)
English writer

Bury me where the birds will sing over my grave.

—ALEXANDER WILSON (1766–1813)
American ornithologist

I never for a day gave up listening to the songs of our birds...
—JOHN JAMES AUDUBON (1785–1851)
American ornithologist

Birds, the free tenants of land, air, and ocean,
Their forms all symmetry, their motions grace....

—JAMES MONTGOMERY (1771–1854)
British poet

Sweet is the breath of morn, her rising sweet with charm of earliest birds.

—JOHN MILTON (1608–1674)
English poet

. . . that rich, delicious, soft, and yet clear music was distinctly heard long after the bird was out of sight.

—JOHN MUIR (1838–1914)
American naturalist

We never miss the music till the sweet-voiced bird has flown.

—O. HENRY (1862–1910)
American writer

When the other birds are still the screech owls take up the strain... Wise midnight hags!... Yet I love to hear their wailing...

HENRY DAVID THOREAU (1817–1862)
American writer and naturalist

I watch in the morning when I wake up. . . . a blackbird. . . . He seems as if his singing were a sort of talking to himself, or of thinking aloud his strongest thoughts. I wish I was a blackbird, like him.

—D.H. LAWRENCE (1885–1930)
English writer

. . . honoring heaven, the bird
traverses
the transparency, without soiling the day.
—PABLO NERUDA (1904–1973)
Chilean poet and diplomat

The idling pivot of the frigate bird
Sways the world's scales, tilts cobalt sea and sky. . .

—DEREK WALCOTT, b. 1930
West Indian writer

There is no square mile of the surface of our planet, wet or dry, that has not been crossed by the shadow of a bird—except, perhaps, parts of the Antarctic continent.

—ROGER TORY PETERSON, b. 1908
American ornithologist and writer
and JAMES FISHER (1912–1970)
English ornithologist and writer

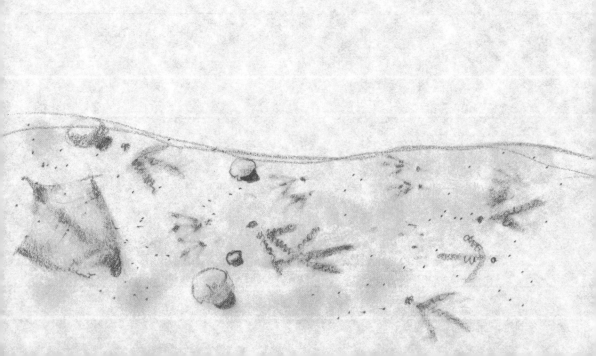

There is nothing in which the birds differ more from man than the way in which they can build and yet leave a landscape as it was before.

—ROBERT LYND (1879–1949)
Irish journalist

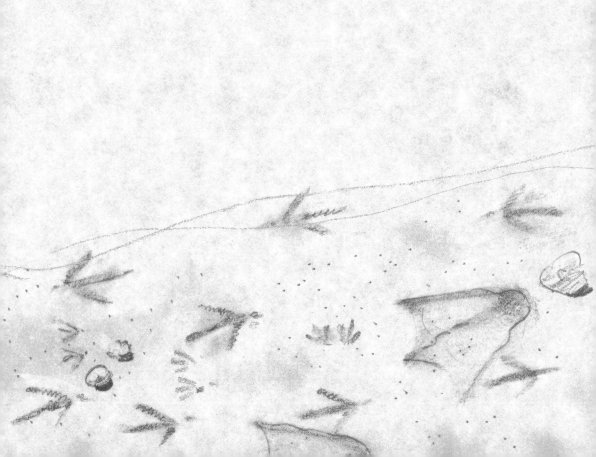

The greater the efforts we make to fathom the secrets of the birds, the more our knowledge expands, the clearer becomes our realization that the secrets of the birds will remain mysteries...

—HANS DOSSENBACH, b. 1936
German illustrator

Learning the secret of flight from a bird was a good deal like learning the secret of magic from a magician. After you once know the trick and know what to look for you see things that you did not notice when you did not know exactly what to look for.

—ORVILLE WRIGHT (1871–1948)
American aviator

It is ironic. . . that despite his intense study of birds, man did not really learn the basic secret of their flight, for the bases of bird-flight remained mysterious long after man had mastered the air.

—CLARENCE D. CONE, JR.
20th-century American biophysicist

Some of us, whether hawks or doves, forceful or peaceful, get up with the birds, swallow a quick breakfast—"not enough to keep a sparrow healthy"—and fly to the station, wondering why the old coot ahead of us doesn't drive more carefully.

—WILLIAM MORRIS
20th-century American editor and writer

The canary has an undulating flight. It flies up into an almost stall, then loops down, then up to a stall and down. It's like Tarzan swinging through the trees but without vines. It's the way I'd like to fly.

—WILLIAM WHARTON
20th-century American writer

*Seagulls, as you know, never falter, never stall. To stall in the air
is for them disgrace and it is dishonor.*

—RICHARD BACH, b. 1936
American writer

Ravens, cockatoos and buzzards fly for the pleasure of it, and playfully enjoy the fullness of their ability.

—KONRAD Z. LORENZ, b. 1903
Austrian ethologist and writer

Everything about a hummingbird is a superlative.
—TOM COLAZO
20th-century American naturalist

I find penguins at present the only comfort in life. One feels everything in the world so sympathetically ridiculous; one can't be angry when one looks at a penguin.

—JOHN RUSKIN (1819–1900)
English art critic and writer

The little flock [of sanderlings] wheeled out over the bay in a wide circle, flashing white wing bars; they returned, crying loudly as they passed over the flats where the young were still running and probing at the edge of the curling wavelets; they turned their heads to the south and were gone.

—RACHEL CARSON (1907–1964)
American biologist and writer

The owl, that bird of onomatopoetic name, is a repetitious question wrapped in feathery insulation especially for winter delivery.

—HAL BORLAND, (1900–1978)
American journalist

I rejoice that there are owls. Let them do the idiotic and maniacal hooting for men. . . . They represent the stark twilight and unsatisfied thoughts which all have.

—HENRY DAVID THOREAU (1817–1862)
American writer and naturalist

Caged birds accept each other but flight is what they long for.

—TENNESSEE WILLIAMS (1914–1983)
American playwright

Watching a former patient soar into the air is the best reward for helping a bird.

—ARLINE THOMAS, b. 1913
American writer

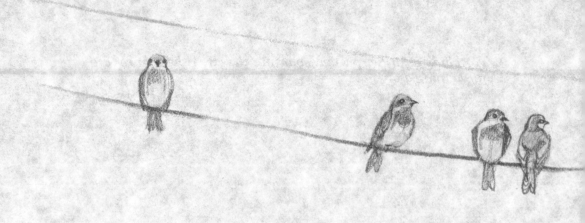

A bird thinks nothing of its flying or it would fall.
—LESLIE SAHLER, b. 1952
American writer

He was flying now straight down, at two hundred fourteen
miles per hour. He swallowed, knowing that if his wings unfold-
ed at that speed he'd be blown into a million tiny shreds of
seagull. But the speed was joy, and the speed was pure beauty.

—RICHARD BACH, b. 1936
American writer

*I am a student of birds. I like to draw birds, and I like to write.
That's enough.*

—GEORGE MIKSCH SUTTON (1898–1982)
American ornithologist

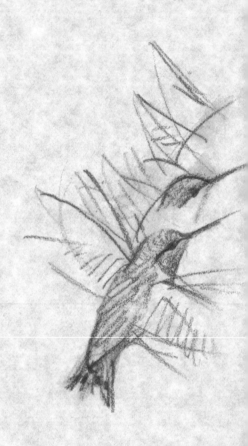

*[The] wren is loudest, longest, most kamikaze when one passes
too near on the way to the mailbox, twittering and hissing as if
one were no better than the neighbor's pink cat. I've always
thought fury a useful passion, given a perilous world.*

—DAVID HOPES, b. 1953
American professor, writer, and poet

... *no two Robins sing their morning carol in exactly the same way.*

—LEN EISERER, b. 1948
American writer and professor of psychology

For some reason the first robin of spring always seems to be alone.

—RICHARD HEADSTROM, b. 1902
American writer and educator

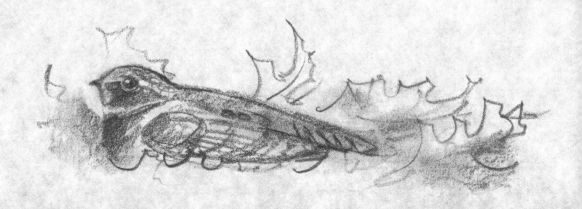

Swans have an air of being proud, stupid, and mischievous—
three qualities that go well together.

—DENIS DIDEROT (1713–1784)
French philosopher

Cheerfulness is proper to the cock, which rejoices over every little thing, and crows with varied and lively movements.

—LEONARDO DA VINCI (1452–1519)
Italian artist

The pigeon is a kind of Quaker. She dresses in grey. . . . No pigeon has ever committed an act of aggression nor turned upon her persecutors: but no bird, likewise, is so skilful in eluding them.

—T.H. WHITE (1906–1964)
English writer

No bird sits on a tree more proudly than a pigeon. It looks as though placed there by the Lord.

—KATHERINE MANSFIELD (1888–1924)
English writer

Seagulls. . . slim yachts of the element.
—ROBINSON JEFFERS (1887–1962)
American poet

I think more of a bird with broad wings flying and lapsing through the air, than anything, when I think of metre.

—D.H. LAWRENCE (1885–1930)
English writer

The blue jay. . . . appears to be among his fellow musicians what the trumpeter is in a band. . . . When disposed for ridicule, there is scarce a bird whose peculiarities of song he cannot tune his notes to. When engaged in the blandishments of love, they resemble the soft chatterings of a duck.

—ALEXANDER WILSON (1766–1813)
Scottish-American ornithologist

*I've never heard a blue jay use bad grammar, but very seldom;
and when they do, they are as ashamed as a human.*

—MARK TWAIN (1835–1910)
American writer

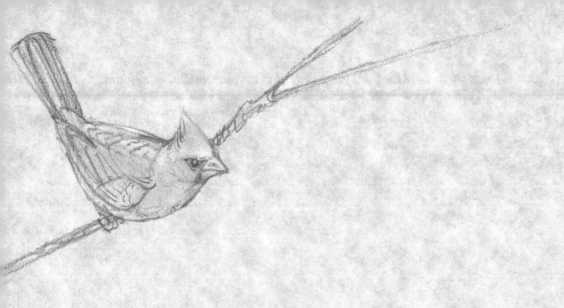

...the skylark warbles high
His trembling thrilling ecstasy;
And, lessening from the dazzled sight,
Melts into air and liquid light.

—THOMAS GRAY (1716–1771)
English poet

How can anyone who is sensitive to birdsong sleep while a mockingbird sings all night outside his window?

—ROGER BARTON (1903–1976)
American writer and lecturer

Solitary the thrush,
The hermit withdrawn to himself, avoiding the settlements,
Sings by himself a song.

—WALT WHITMAN (1819–1892)
American poet

That's the wise thrush; he sings each song twice over
Lest you should think he never could recapture
The first fine careless rapture!

—ROBERT BROWNING (1812–1889)
English poet

The thrush is busy in the wood,
And carols loud and strong.

—WILLIAM WORDSWORTH (1770–1850)
English poet

The songs of the birds were so pleasant that it seemed as if a man could never wish to leave the place. The flocks of parrots concealed the sun; and the birds were so numerous, and of so many different kinds, that it was wonderful.

—CHRISTOPHER COLUMBUS (1451–1506)
Spanish explorer

One swallow doesn't make a summer, but too many swallows make a fall.

—GEORGE D. PRENTICE (1802–1870)
American journalist and humorist

It was early September, a red bright day of Indian summer sun and stillness, and the beach bird stood immobile for a time, observing the turtles and a muskrat, two black ducks and a green heron, as if certain of its central place in a strange and beautiful universe.

—PETER MATTHIESSEN, b. 1927
American naturalist and writer

*In their idealization of the eagle, people have made it represen-
tative of power, courage, conquest, freedom, independence,
magnanimity, truth, and immortality.*

—TOM EVANS
20th-century American writer

I respond very positively to certain birds. Especially eagles; and now I know from my experiences in dreams that at some time in my past life I have been a bird of that particular kind, because I know exactly the feeling of flying and living in the body of that bird.

—KARLHEINZ STOCKHAUSEN, b. 1928
German composer and conductor

*And now for the eagle! I hate to shatter the fabulous illusions
about this glorious bird, but I must adhere to the truth: all
true birds of prey are, compared with passerines or parrots,
extremely stupid creatures. . . . This, of course, does not preclude
this proud bird from being beautiful and impressive and
embodying the very essence of wild life. . . .*

—KONRAD Z. LORENZ, b. 1903
Austrian ethologist and writer

I wish the bald eagle had not been chosen as the representative of our country, he is a bird of bad moral character. . . . The turkey is a much more respectable bird, and withal a true original native of America.

—BENJAMIN FRANKLIN (1706–1790)
American statesman and writer

Whatever the bird is, is perfect in the bird.

—JUDITH WRIGHT, b. 1915
Australian poet and critic

In a world that seems so very puzzling is it any wonder birds have such appeal? Birds are, perhaps, the most eloquent expression of reality.

—ROGER TORY PETERSON, b. 1908
American ornithologist

He prayeth well, who loveth well
Both man and bird and beast.

—SAMUEL TAYLOR COLERIDGE (1772–1834)
English poet and critic

I have looked upon those brilliant creatures,
And now my heart is sore.

—WILLIAM BUTLER YEATS (1865–1939)
Irish poet and dramatist

Although birds coexist with us on this eroded planet, they live independently of us with a self-sufficiency that is almost a rebuke.

—BROOKS ATKINSON (1894–1984)
American critic

The truth of the matter is, the birds could very well live without us, but many—perhaps all—of us would find life incomplete, indeed almost intolerable without the birds.

—ROGER TORY PETERSON, b. 1908
American ornithologist

A holy of holies for me was the tower of the big building on the
Cotner campus. Here, after the climb on all fours up a rickety
ramp, I could count on seeing two barn owls.

—GEORGE MIKSCH SUTTON (1898–1982)
American ornithologist

Parakeets...are good pets.... [They] do not ruin the
neighbor's grass...or need to be walked on cold nights, or bite
the mailman, or scratch the furniture.

—BARBARA M. VAYO
20th-century American writer

Nobody has any sympathy for a hen because she is not beautiful; while everyone gets sentimental over the oriole and says how shocking to kill the lovely thing.

—DON MARQUIS (1878–1937)
American journalist

Many things people do harm birds much more that hunting.
—IRA N. GABRIELSON (1889–1977)
American naturalist

Are we never to realize and admit that our most sincere reason for protecting the birds is simply that we want them as they are about us. . . .

—GEORGE MIKSCH SUTTON (1898–1982)
American ornithologist

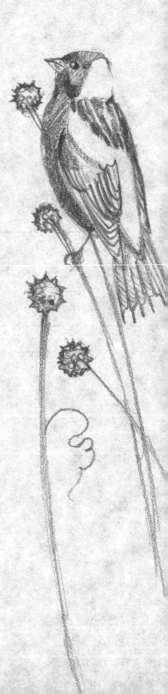

When you have shot one bird flying you have shot all birds flying.

—ERNEST HEMINGWAY (1899–1961)
American writer

Nothing wholly admirable ever happens in this country except the migration of birds.

—BROOKS ATKINSON (1894–1984)
American critic

*The wild goose comes north with the voice of freedom and
adventure. He is more than a big, far-ranging bird; he is the
epitome of wanderlust, limitless horizons and distant travel. He
is the yearning and the dream, the search and the wonder, the
unfettered foot and the wind's will wing.*

—HAL BORLAND (1900–1978)
American journalist

Did you ever chance to hear the midnight flight of birds passing through the air and darkness overhead, in countless armies, changing their early, or late summer habitat? It is something not to be forgotten....

—WALT WHITMAN (1819–1892)
American poet

. . . *I dreamed last night. . . . I felt the music before I heard it. I*
was myself the wren, singing at dawn in Paradise. I've searched
remembrance for a better dream; and I keep searching.

—DAVID HOPES, b. 1953
American professor, writer, and poet

Without birds, where would we have learned that there can be a song in the heart?

—HAL BORLAND (1900–1978)
American journalist